D1521682

the field of why

Yavanika Press

the field of why

Cover Design & Interior Images: Shloka Shankar

First published in 2022 by Yavanika Press
Bangalore, India

ISBN: 9798427871860

For every single one of you who has shown me kindness.

Acknowledgements

I was introduced to contemporary English Language haiku by Kashinath Karmakar, Kala Ramesh, Vinay Leo R., and several others in the winter of 2013 when I joined INhaiku (now Triveni Haikai India), a secret workshopping group on Facebook. Soon, I set out to discover and unravel the joyous world of haikai literature and was instantly smitten by haiku, senryu, and haiga in particular. I would like to thank Kala and all my fellow poets at Triveni for providing a nurturing environment for my growth as both writer and editor over the years.

the field of why is my debut full-length collection of 51 poems that span nearly a decade and explore my preoccupation with such themes as identity, belonging, language, relationships, and my disability, among others. The book you are now holding in your hands has gone through various stages of evolution and the one constant has been my dearest friend and co-editor, Robin Anna Smith, who helped screen over half a dozen versions since 2019. Their monumental patience and thorough understanding of my craft and voice was a huge plus for me when I found myself washed over by waves of imposter syndrome or refusing to believe I was "ready". Their faith in me remains unwavering, and, for that, I will forever be grateful.

The few loose ends in the structure of my book were brought to my attention by fellow poet, friend, and co-editor Kat Lehmann. Thank you, Kat, for painstakingly reviewing my manuscript and for your excellent, perceptive inputs.

I also extend my heartfelt gratitude to fellow poet and birthday twin Ashish Narain, for writing an honest, kind, and thoughtful blurb.

In recent years, Rohan Kevin Broach has played a pivotal part in my journey by being my go-to person for everything related to technology. Rohan, whom I fondly rechristened Magic Hands, thanks a god zillion for everything. *the field of why* marks Yavanika Press' fiftieth title, and we could not have reached this milestone without you.

To the scores of editors who have encouraged and polished my work, a million thank-yous. A significant number of poems in this collection first appeared in the following venues:

A Hundred Gourds, All the Way Home: Aging in Haiku (ed. Robert Epstein, 2019), *ant ant ant ant ant, bones: a journal for the short poem, Failed Haiku, Frameless Sky, FreshOut Mag, Frogpond, Hedgerow: A Journal of Small Poems, Heliosparrow, NOON: Journal of the Short Poem, Otata, Otoliths, Prune Juice,* The Haiku Sanctuary Kukai (March 2020), *the other bunny, The Zen Space, Under the Basho, Wales Haiku Journal, Weird Laburnum, whiptail: journal of the single-line poem,* and *Whispers.*

I owe my parents, family, and close friends a deep bow of gratitude for helping me birth my literary baby into the world. Thank you for your invaluable support.

"He who has a why to live for can bear almost any how."

— Friedrich Nietzsche

the field of why

working material until Brahma created light

cutting into the envelope :: the grand narrative of being

walking to think I happened

in media res the dreamscape of our lives

ruined

          I manufacture

by a set

          comet trails

of influences

          of fancy

balancing darkness a poem with birds in it

pulling sins out of a dreamer conscience

the days I pluck a mute destiny

ivory tower shadows of loneliness

the routine of memory in a windowless room

a tittle-t
w, there
d chaffir
ll water
did not
for c
an
rever
esid
, a kr
poor
ded
can
s
ed r
e d
he
d t
rim
sh

folding a handkerchief my anxiety of influence

empty for the moment until whenever

mor
ning depre
ciates
into
a Wed
nesday
after
noon sever
al times

2:1 the echo of reason fading

filed under miscellaneous the will to live

set for the comedy that never comes :: water remains water

asking me where I am Polaris

where losing becomes loss silver wind

crepuscular this longing for

flour in the air :: dissertations on fate

getting to the core of a spartan afterthought

sutradhara
the things I can't
control

bcc'ing myself from myself from

my internal machinery—
flashbacks become flash forwards

almost
dusk
I
confront
my
otherness

penumbra the side of me you

ableism

the narrative

of stairs

fitting my body into a yawn

ipso facto who's waving and who's drowning?

in my bones the dimness of someone else's voice

falling from trees a blueprint for the unsaid

desaturat**ing** the moment your

with nowhere to go words collect in the tympanum

examining the nails of vowels so quiet, so old

space-time continuum :: we become each other's soliloquies

black cinder I must learn to talk

erecting landmarks in the field of why

one-third of my past soars on Garuda's wing

self-validation
raindrops on a telephone wire

either/or
relapse into
a coda

the sheen on an orange rind negative capability

staying
on the bus

I am

the
refrain

as an aside I shape-shift into a key

open boxes—

I want to know if
you believe

a prototype of courage amidst winter stars

breaking through the gender of happiness

spring rain…
soon, we become
our own gods

tomorrow in a gathering of elsewhere

mango blossom…
what if every day was
a red-letter day

aubade—
your hands hold up
my sky

(*for my mother*)

before and after the wasteland white butterflies

Shloka Shankar is a poet, editor, publisher, and self-taught visual artist from Bangalore, India. She enjoys experimenting with Japanese short-forms and myriad found poetry techniques alike. A Best of the Net nominee and award-winning haiku poet, her poems and artwork have appeared in over 200 online and print venues of repute. In addition, she has edited and co-edited six international poetry anthologies since 2016. Shloka is the Founding Editor of the literary & arts journal *Sonic Boom* and its imprint Yavanika Press. When she isn't poring over manuscripts, you can find her making abstract art, digital collages, or conducting poetry workshops. Shloka is the author of the microchap *Points of Arrival* (Origami Poems Project, 2021).

Website: www.shlokashankar.com

Made in the USA
Coppell, TX
18 May 2022